On

Western Shores

by PJ Collings

The Songster's House

Published in 2015 by: The Songster's House,
Ballybofey, Co. Donegal, Ireland.
www.thesongstershouse.ie

ISBN 978-0-9933125-0-2

Acknowledgements:
Thanks go first and foremost to Billy Patton for his invaluable contribution to
this publication and for his unstinting support. Not only has he provided the
guitar chord accompaniment to all the songs but he has brought the tunes to
life with his fiddle playing, took numerous photographs and even wielded a
paintbrush for some of the illustrations. Thanks to Nuala for her beautiful
painting that she has allowed us to use for the cover page, to Musescore for
providing such good music notation freeware, to PJ's song-writing pals Jacqui
and Karen for inspiring her in the first place, and to John and Julia for
cheering us on! Special thanks go to Jenny Swann, editor at Candlestick Press,
for her support, ideas and scones.

On Western Shores is dedicated to Mama Mia Collings, who never gives up
and who is PJ's first and most optimistic supporter.

Printed in Donegal by Browne Printers Ltd
tel. 074 9121387
www.browneprinters.com

Foreword

How does a songwriter who doesn't enjoy performing share her songs?

This is the question that has led to the publication of *On Western Shores*, an original collection of songs and tunes that will provide singers and musicians with new material to experiment with, and visitors to Ireland with a unique souvenir of their time here. It is also intended as a celebration of the North West of Ireland for the people who live here.

Whether or not you read or play music, we hope you'll enjoy the stories that go with each piece. These give an insight into the ideas behind the writing of the songs, while the free demo CD means you can listen and learn by ear from our (literally!) 'recorded-in-the-kitchen' versions.

Index of Songs and Tunes

1. All Rivers Run

You don't need to spend a lot of time in this North Western corner of Ireland to know that rivers and streams, shucks and ditches, burns and loughs and waterfalls have a major impact on the character of the landscape.

Drainage of the rain-soaked land is a constant challenge for these watercourses, continually fed by the rains coming in from the Atlantic seaboard. Of course, they also provide fantastic habitats for some of the iconic species of the area, many of which I've been lucky enough to see, though as yet the kingfisher is not one of them – one day maybe.

A few years ago I returned to study and learned all about the mechanics of the water cycle. I liked the notion that the glass of water I drink today may once have been part of a vast ocean, a frozen glacier, a cloud, or even a faraway person's tears.

This song celebrates the wonders of that immense global cycle and the way it links us all together, along with the beauty of the rivers it has produced in this particular landscape. Long may they run.

All Rivers Run

D minor

Instrumental

Sing Freely **Dm**

All Ri-vers run, all ri-vers run, all ri-vers run, all ri-vers run, all ri-vers run, all ri-vers flow down to the sea.

Instrumental

High in the hills up from the depths e-rupts a spring, a cen-tury's dream to steal the light, a sil-ver thread a run-ning stream. It tum-bles wild and roam-ing, joy-ous to be free.

And where a stream flows light and fast, the salmon leap, kingfishers flash,
A dipper dips, the waters gather broad and deep.
There, dragonflies emerge above the calm and gleam.

Beyond a bend, the river pauses, takes a breath and wanders on,
It's deep and dark and barely still, it looks like trees.
It looks like skies, this trick of light, just a disguise.

A tumbling sky, the river roars, it's wearing white beneath the noise,
It swells and soars, it's breaking banks, devouring sward.
Leaves in its wake a soft dark silt, the soil's reward.

And when you cry, your salty teardrops fade and dry, then they may rise
Into the sky where they form clouds that toss and turn.
Until they fall again as raindrops on the land.

All rivers run, all rivers run, all rivers run, all rivers run, all rivers run,
All rivers flow down to the sea.

2. Mountains in my Mind

Although I've only lived in Donegal for twenty years and am therefore still officially a 'blow-in', i.e. someone who has arrived from outside of the county, its landscape and in particular the mountains and hills around me have entered my soul.

That first glimpse of the Gap at Barnesmore, part of the Bluestack mountain range, or the Sperrin Mountains that stretch inland from County Tyrone, or the splendid sights of Muckish (which I have climbed) and Errigal (which I haven't, yet...) are always a welcome sight when I return home after a tiring journey. Travelling south from Donegal town it is the Dartry mountain range, which includes the famous Ben Bulben, that dominates the view along the coast to Sligo.

The patchwork of field, bog, and forestry and the incredible effects that come with the varieties of light and shade experienced in this part of the world will be familiar to anyone lucky enough to venture here, and no wonder they inspire so many photographers and landscape artists.

The thought of leaving this rugged mountainous landscape behind, something I have been contemplating for a while, inspired the writing of this song.

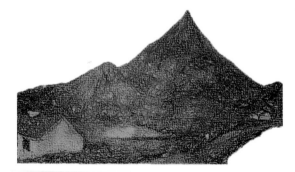

Mountains In My Mind

C minor

You are the most extraordinary sight,
You've cradled me for years,
Though aeons pass, your watch stands still,
You barely know I'm here.
But how I'll miss you.
Though we've scarred your sides
You will override all the harm that we can do,
You're a timeline in the sky,
Marking ages all the while,
In your ancient rock-hewn robes.
If never I return again,
I'll keep these mountains in my mind.

You are the most extraordinary sight,
I've watched you disappear
'Neath milk-white mists, or lead-grey clouds,
Or ink black starlit skies,
And how I'll miss you.
When you're barely there, floating in mid-air,
I sense your presence still,
You're a whisper in the sky
Hearing all our weary sighs,
In your washed out linen robes.
If never I return again,
I'll keep these mountains in my mind.

Whenever I return again, I'll see these mountains in your eyes.

3. Parade

Surely the miles walked and danced by all the hundreds of participants in festival parades throughout Ireland each year would stretch many times the length of the country from Dingle to Donaghadee? I wrote this tune for fiddle to celebrate the mass of colour and movement that these diverse and cheery parades bring to towns from early Spring to late Autumn whether in bright sunshine or in pouring rain.

4. Digging the Spuds

There's a saying: "There's not much they can do to you once you have your spuds in for the year" and so we grow our own potatoes, but also because they are just delicious straight from the ground. The digging of the first spuds of the year, revealing bright gold or red nuggets clustered together in the dark earth, never fails to excite. Then we spoil it by sticking a tine of the fork through the biggest most perfect spud of the lot … There's a rhythm to the digging once you get going though, fork in, shuggle up, turn over, start again, which underpins this next tune for fiddle.

It should ideally be played while the first dish of steaming spuds, cooked until the skins just start to split, revealing the flesh beneath, is brought to a table adorned simply with a pot of salt, a large wodge of yellow Irish butter and bright green scallions. Dig in!

Parade

C major

Digging the Spuds

B minor

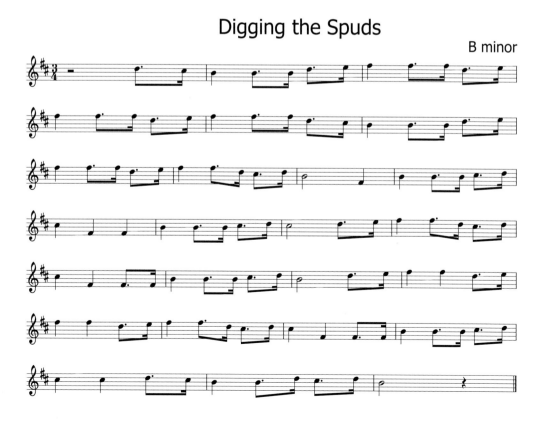

5. The Rob Roy

My partner, Billy, has spent many hours researching the truth behind a story he'd heard surrounding his family history and a small boat called The Rob Roy. He carefully pieced together the recollections of family members, newspaper accounts and oral history records from the Folklore Commission's School project. He discovered that his great, great grandfather, his great grandfather and his first cousin twice removed had all perished at sea on December 21st 1894, the night of the biggest storm to hit Ireland since the night of the Big Wind in 1839. All three men were named James. They were sailing a boat known as a lugger, the Rob Roy, from Buncrana down Lough Swilly, with a fifty ton load of sand on board, destined for the building of Letterkenny Cathedral.

I wrote this song for Billy and his family in remembrance of that tragedy. It is sung from the imagined perspective of his great, great Grandmother, about whom nothing is known at the present time.

The Rob Roy

D major

Verse lyrics (under the staves):

On the shor-test day, in the year of nine-ty four, my three James-es set to
-edral's going up and they need a load of sand, we'll take the Rob Roy to Bun-

sea, They were pi-lots all, from the shores of Do-ne-gal, three gen-er-
crana, We'll get her floating at high tide, and we'll make the trip to-night, we'll have our-

a-tions of my fa-mi-ly. And the wind rose up and the rain came down and the
selves a prop-er Christ-mas dinner."

waves rolled o-ver the prow, "There's a storm a-com-ing up lads but it's
"We'll make it in-to port lads with our

no-thing much to fear, one more job will see us through to the New Year". "The cath-
fif-ty tonnes of sand, for the Rob Roy's the best lug-ger in the land".

They worked hard with little rest,
Knew Lough Swilly just the best,
And they'd tease us for our worry.
"It couldn't drown us if it tried,"
They would joke and jest with pride,
"There's more water in your cup of tea!"
And the wind rose up and the rain came down,
And the waves rolled over the prow,
"It's a proper dirty night lads
And the waves are getting high,
But we'll make it to the port before sunrise."

We stayed up all night
As the gale began to roar
With a fury never heard before,
Through the din and crash,
All we thought of was our lads,
Tossed and buffeted like feathers by the shore.
And the wind rose up and the rain came down
And the waves crashed over the prow,
"We'd best try to get to shore lads -
Pull the punt up to the fore,
We'll leave this load of sand behind now."

All the lights went out,
Just before the midnight hour,
That tempest lifted roofs from houses,
The destruction wrought by that deadly storm
Left devastation all around us,
And the wind rose up and the rain came down,
And the waves crashed over the prow,
And the sand was drenched
And the lugger went down,
And my three brave Jameses can't be found.

Now it's three months on,
We've just buried my boy
Near the body of my grandson James.
But my dear one lies
Cold and lifeless with no grave,
near the bare bones of the old Rob Roy.
And the wind rose up and the rain came down,
And the waves crashed over the prow,
And the sand was drenched,
And the lugger went down,
And my three brave Jameses were all drowned.

And the sand was drenched,
And the lugger went down,
And my own dear James was never found.

6. The Story of a Lifetime

I work in a small library serving a rural town and villages in County Tyrone, where I've had the privilege of gradually getting to know the many regular visitors. Often through short conversations held over the course of several years, and very often about our favourite topic, the weather! But also through peoples' choice of reading material, the books I have read, the authors people like, the authors they don't like, recommendations for a good read that are a big hit and those that fall flat...

Among these visitors is a remarkable couple, both of them are great readers, they visit the library every week almost without fail, and they are quite obviously devoted to one another. Both are in their late eighties and a few years ago they celebrated their Ruby Wedding Anniversary. I couldn't help but draw a parallel between their shared lives and two volumes of one story, beautifully bound in leather and standing proud. A sixty year marriage is a rare thing. This song was written for them.

The Story of a Lifetime

B♭ Major

Chorus

They are two vol·umes of one sto·ry, They stand to·geth·er side by

side, each page well·thumbed, the co·vers gleam·ing with the pa·ti·na of age. It is the

sto·ry of a life·time, and though their dan·cing days are done, She's still his
ac·res of po·ta·toes, she's made a thou·sand pots of jam, They've grown a

Babs, and he's her Bob·bie·o and their love is bold__ and__ strong, and their
fam·ily and a fo·rest too, in the sha·dow of__ the__ hill, in the

love is bold and strong.
sha·dow of the hill.

2.He's plan·ted

He rises early every morning,
To measure sunshine, wind and rain,
She's woven shawls that fall like gossamer
'Round the forms of newborn babes.
Around the forms of newborn babes.

They're neither rich, and they're not famous,
And yet they've surely made their mark,
They've seen some sights we'll never see again,
Sung some songs we've never heard.
They've sung some songs we've never heard.

They are two volumes of one story,
They stand together, side by side,
Each page well-thumbed, the covers gleaming
With the patina of age.
It is the story of a lifetime,
And though their dancing days are done,
She's still his Babs and he's her Bobby-o,
And their love is bold and strong,
And their love is bold and strong.

7. The Grave Digger

When my partner and I arrived in Ireland in 1994 it was a different place, for better or worse. Pre Celtic Tiger, the local pubs became our social hub and were full of chat and music, and above all, full of characters. Sadly, many of them have since passed away, among them a grave digger who became a good friend of ours over the years. We spent many an evening in his company in his favourite pub, talking, laughing and singing, and later on it was our privilege to visit him at home and finally in the Donegal hospice.

When I heard a programme on the radio about grave diggers, highlighting the dwindling tradition of digging graves by hand, and the special characteristics of the people who take on this role, I was reminded of that lovely man.

A bit of googling revealed that surprisingly few songs have been written about this profession, so I wrote this one in his memory. Suffice it to say that he had a good sense of humour! Cheers C.

The Grave Digger

G minor

You'd dig with strength and you'd dig with pride,
Three feet wide and nice straight sides,
You'd keep on digging till the job was done
When you'd be standing at the bottom
Of a six foot tomb.
Chorus

You lived your whole life in this wee small town,
You knew all the families for miles around,
You'd dig for anyone who wanted you to,
Though it wasn't always easy,
You'd see it through.
Chorus

When you've dealt with the other-world
All your life,
It's no surprise you'd enjoy a pint!
When the craic was good and your pipe was full,
You'd sing and yarn
The whole night through.
Chorus

When your luck ran out, you didn't give in,
You kept on living to the very end,
But there'd be no more digging
For those two strong arms,
No more singing, no more yarns.
Chorus

Who dug your grave? I cannot say,
But you'd be glad to know
They did it your way,
Three feet wide and nice straight sides,
Six feet down and finished with pride.

Digging on down, down, down,
Digging on down.
Digging on down, down, down,
Digging on down. Digging on down.

8. The Pullyarney Bogslide

The phenomenon of the bogslide will be unfamiliar to many – it is a rare and sometimes devastating occurrence when an entire section of blanket bog becomes detached from the bedrock on which it has lain for millennia and slides, wholescale, downhill. This event occurred in November 1900, in the townland of Pullyarney in County Tyrone not far from our own home in Donegal. Though local roads were covered and homes needed to be dug out from beneath several metres of sodden peat, nobody was injured and the story has become a local legend.

9. The Barn Beside the House

This is the tune that waltzed off on its own when I was writing the song that became 'At Ben Bulben's Side'. Since it came home to roost, and because this house with its stone outbuildings and its one acre have been such an important part of my life for the past 18 years, I had to dedicate this dance tune to the two-storey barn that sits at right angles to the house. When this house was in its heyday, with a farm of land attached, it was apparently a popular raking (meeting) house and dances were often held in the hayloft. Nowadays it provides a cool dark place to store the spuds over winter, and is home to starlings, jackdaws and swallows in spring, who bring their own version of music to the party.

The Pullyarney Bogslide

D major

The Barn Beside the House

C major

10. On Knocknarea

Just outside Sligo on the road out to the sea, stands the unmistakeable form of Knocknarea mountain, topped with a giant cairn of stones, placed there, it is said, to mark a grave, and continually added to by the many people who climb up to admire the expansive view. The grave is over 2000 years old and is said to be that of Queen Maeve of Connaught, best known for her role in the famous story of the 'Táin Bó Cúailnge', the 'Cattle Raid of Cooley'.

What a good idea to fête her in song, this great woman, a Queen in her own right, as powerful as any King, mother to at least seven sons and a daughter, and an inspiration to the early Celtic scribes.

But ...on further reading it turns out that it's not certain as to whether Maeve's existence is historically accurate or pure legend, and County Roscommon also lays claim to her final resting place. The other *slight* problem is that she was a scheming warmonger who had her own sister killed, not necessarily something I want to celebrate...

How to proceed? Well, there are many more questions about Queen Maeve than answers, and the lesson from the 'Cattle Raid of Cooley' is still relevant today. War is never the best way to resolve an argument.

On Knocknarea?

D minor

Is Queen Maeve here on Knock-na-rea, be-neath this crown of stone

Is it myth or is it his-to-ry, says here lie royal bones? Can it have

been two thou-sand years, for so the sto-ries tell Since her sons and

daugh-ter shed their tears, when their own mo-ther fell?

The raven and the squirrel passed
Maeve's stories down the line,
Ten centuries in the telling
Until men wrote them down.

Was Maeve so proud, so vain, so keen,
To prove her husband poor,
That she vowed to send her armies forth
To wage a jealous war?

Was she prepared to risk the lives
Of several hundred men,
For to raid the Cooley Mountain Range
And bring that Brown Bull hence?

What did Maeve say
When that Brown Bull,
Was brought before her throne,
When it killed the mighty white horned bull,
Then fled to die at home?

Instrumental

What were Maeve's thoughts that day
She bathed, on Inis Cloithreann's shores,
Remorse for killing kith and kin,
Or plans to wage more wars?

The raven and the squirrel saw
The shot that brought her down,
In revenge for his young mother's death,
Maeve's nephew sought her crown.

So whether truth or myth is known,
Look out from Knocknarea,
And know that wars are never won
On land or out at sea.

And know that wars are never won
On land or out at sea.

11. At Ben Bulben's Side

I've written of mountains in another song in this collection but I had to write Ben Bulben a song of its own – anyone who has seen this most impressive slab of a mountain, known locally as Sligo's very own Table Mountain, will surely remember it.

Writing a song about a mountain isn't as easy as it sounds, even the tune I had started to put together split itself in two as I tried to find a starting point - the other half waltzed off on its own to become the tune for 'The Barn Beside the House'!

I especially wanted to capture some of the drama that light and shade bring to the party and how the whole mountain changes shape entirely as you travel around it. And I wanted to convey something of the sense of time passing as a landscape is viewed, an image that can't be fixed or experienced any other way than by being there at that moment in time, looking on.

Also, it was absolutely impossible to ignore the voice of W.B. Yeats who famously lies buried in Drumcliff graveyard at the foot of the mountain, at his own request, as outlined in his poem 'Under Ben Bulben'.

At Ben Bulben's Side

C minor

As the light fan-tas-tic trips a-long the hill-top of Ben - bul__ben From the
ear-ly morn-ing ris-ing to the sink-ing of the sun As each fleet-ing i-mage
glan-ces off the sheer drop of the moun-tain, Here the po-et's words un-
fold this world in verse and lilt-ing song. *Chorus* Tra-vel light a-long the
val__ley, Be__ wise a-long the val-ley Tra-vel deep a-long the val-ley at Ben
Bul - bens__ side

As the sea reveals its secrets, fossils polished by the tide,
Crazy seashells found on mountain tops, in limestone vaults reside,
As the Ancients travel with us, when so hurriedly we stride,
So the poet lays embroidered cloths, our pounding soles to guide.

Chorus

As a cloud that perches softly on the rising crenellations,
As the sunlight shifts a myriad of shadows on each face,
Take your seat at Table Mountain, feast your eyes upon the landscape,
As the horseman passes by, then may the poet keep you safe.

Chorus

As the mountain's a reminder of our place in time and space,
So its height defies its gravity, and depths define the darkness,
Visions vanishing beyond what was the future, as you gaze,
Tread softly as you travel by the poet's resting place.

Chorus

12. On Western Shores

We have a tradition of visiting a beach in Donegal (that shall remain nameless!) every St. Stephen's day to collect a pot of fresh mussels for our tea. Last year we were away for Christmas so we were waiting for a chance in the New Year to make this annual sandy pilgrimage. On a not-very-promising Sunday afternoon in January, grey and cool and windy, but dry at least, we decided on the spur of the moment to risk a trip out to the coast – no camera, no picnic, just warm coats and gloves. We drove through the Barnesmore Gap into a perfectly clear and sunny winter's afternoon. The tide was in, so the mussel beach was out of bounds, we headed instead for Murvagh strand, where, after finding our way through the newly created forest walk, we emerged at the far car park to walk back along the beach.

This song tries (and fails!) to capture that half hour of sheer bliss.

On Western Shores
(On Murvagh Beach in January)

F major

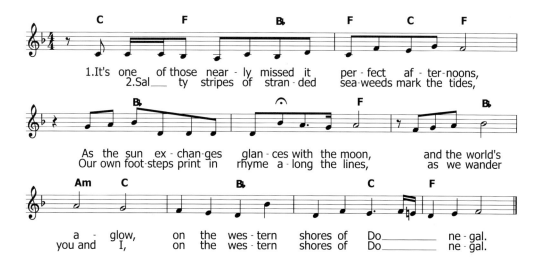

1.It's one of those near - ly missed it per - fect af - ter-noons,
2.Sal___ ty stripes of stran - ded sea-weeds mark the tides,

As the sun ex - chan-ges glan - ces with the moon, and the world's
Our own foot-steps print in rhyme a - long the lines, as we wander

a - glow, on the wes - tern shores of Do_____ ne - gal.
you and I, on the wes - tern shores of Do_____ ne - gal.

Sun-rimmed clouds sketch out new landscapes far away,
And beyond the hills mist rolls in from the bay,
It's a picture postcard day, on the western shores of Donegal.

Waves of silver murmur swansongs on the strand, they leave
A clean slate edged in lace on golden sand,
A new day will be inscribed on the western shores of Donegal.

No lens or pen could ever capture all of this,
So we'll treasure every moment it exists,
Go with the ebb and flow, on the western shores of Donegal.

It's one of those nearly-missed-it perfect afternoons,
As the sun exchanges glances with the moon,
And the world's aglow, on the western shores of Donegal.